# Homesteading Basics: A Proven Guide to Ensuring Sustainable Living and Self-Reliance

Sarah German

©2014 Sarah German

## Table of Contents

Introduction

Chapter 1: Simple Living, Self-Sufficiency, Sustainability

Chapter 2: Different Types of Gardens, & Tips On Incorporating Permaculture & Bio dynamics Into the Landscape

Chapter 3: Preserving Food; Making Bread, Butter and Cheese

Chapter 4: Keeping Small-Scale Livestock (Chickens, Goats, Rabbits); Beekeeping

Chapter 5: Introduction To Probiotic Fermentation

Chapter 6: Water Conservation, Alternative Energy Sources (Energy Independence)

Conclusion

# Introduction

I want to thank you, and congratulate you, for downloading the book Homesteading Basics: A Proven Guide to Ensuring Sustainable Living and Self-Reliance. I am honored to be a part of your learning journey towards self-sufficiency & I can promise you, it will be so much fun!!!

This book contains proven steps and strategies on how to learn the basics of homesteading, as well giving you simple, effective tools to plan & start your own homestead (whether rural or urban), opening you up to a world so completely satisfying, you cannot imagine the possibilities. By the end of this book, you will be well on your way to creating, using & living true, tested, daily ways towards your personal homesteading bliss.

Here's an inescapable fact: Homesteading, as a hobby, a passion, & a way of life, is on the rise for many reasons. Connecting with our food sources, & controlling what goes into our bodies from the beginning of planting time to the finished product, being one of the largest reasons by far. In this modern age of chemical-laden, genetically altered, highly & unnaturally processed, "food-like products", it is all the more important to preserve & bring back the ways & knowledge of how traditional FOOD is grown, harvested, prepared & minimally processed. Imagine your very own delicious, in-season food on the table for your family~ with a taste unparalleled by any other......! Fresh fruits, berries & vegetables, delicious eggs from your own backyard chickens, raw honey from your own bees, soft creamy herbed cheese with milk from your own goats, mixed with herbs from the herb garden.... the list can go on & on as everyone oohs & ahhs in delight!

It also offers us a way to slow down, to breathe in the primal, ancient scent of the earth, reconnect with generations of our forefathers & wise mothers before us, whose wisdom & millennia of experience by trial, error & perfection of all homesteading arts remains, as a vast reserve for all to tap into & learn for ourselves, our families, & each other, to share & trade in a depth & richness you cannot buy from the industrialized world. This wisdom exists beyond what money can buy. It is woven into the very fabric of our being, as our original hunter-gatherer selves, as Natural Man.

As well as personal happiness & fulfillment in nurturing these home & garden projects start to finish, is that most practical application of it all... It is a most useful hobby for certain, the experience & satisfaction of growing & preparing your own foods, fermenting your own drinks, making healing remedies for your family, connecting with the natural world & the rhythm of the earth's seasons so deeply ~ while simultaneously, the end result & larger picture is improved health, longevity, & quality of life for yourself and your loved ones.

Don't feel pressured to learn everything in-depth & all at once, or you may perhaps feel overwhelmed. A more laid-back approach is to choose one or two things to add to your new lifestyle itinerary: once a month, or week, etc. Relax. This is YOUR journey. Choose things that feel best at the time for you to look into more, try out, & in YOUR own time, incorporate into your very own homestead. Thus an ever-changing kaleidoscope of wonderful, new, personalized traditions are born for your family, as you simultaneously anchor more deeply into the very rhythms of the earth itself... Becoming aware of the changing seasons & what they bring to the natural world before fading & giving way to another seasonal delight! It is truly a world of wonder, the Simple Life.

Okay! Commencement time for a fascinating overview, to whet your appetite to begin: living as an industrious protégé of self-sufficiency, traditional down-home ways, ancient wisdom & how-to. These are skills that will stick with you, & whomever YOU then in turn teach them to, for the rest of your life! Come on, let's begin right away!!

# Chapter 1: Simple Living, Self-Sufficiency, Sustainability

The definition of homesteading, according to Wikipedia, is as follows: "Broadly defined, homesteading is a lifestyle of self-sufficiency. It is characterized by subsistence agriculture, home preservation of foodstuffs, and it may or may not also involve the small scale production of textiles, clothing, and craftwork for household use or sale."

"Simple Living" ties in with this when you examine your lifestyle, & weed out things you feel you no longer need, trading them in for a more-favored, less-hectic, more natural vibration closer to Nature & the seasonal gifts she has to offer. Do you really use that overpriced cable subscription you are a slave to, or could you trim it down, or cancel it altogether & use the money to either invest in natural living supplies initially or, (if you are doing everything entirely from scratch like our ancestors did, without much in the way of store-bought equipment) instead save the money from that, and other things, and be able to work a little less in the industrialized "outside world" so you can anchor into, relax and enjoy your homestead more?? Just an idea! Many have left the city in favor of a slower, simpler life on your own dream "hobby farm", a small eco- farmstead/homestead with just enough of everything, for their family to live abundantly, & eat throughout the winter... with freshly preserved foods, and brilliant ways of existing, nay flourishing, outside the box! If you cannot leave the city & find your dream "forest farm retreat" etc., out in the mountains just yet, there are brilliant ways to incorporate many of these wise old practices into the more recently-coined term "Urban Homesteading", right in the city & suburbs.

There are many ways to provide a Simpler Living/Self-Sufficiency blueprint for yourself. With a little research you may find you can do without a LOT of the nonsense! Giving way to what you truly want to do, including revamping the hearth & home to be as sustainable as possible, which to me personally is more exciting than any sitcom or overpriced, temporary fix that many in the first world generally run to for destressing. Don't be afraid to think of creative solutions that work for you, & do a lot of research!!!! Google is absolutely amazing for this~ Look up every buzzword you can think of, and read others' homesteading blogs & stories for ideas & inspiration!

Another excellent Wikipedia citation: "Self-sufficiency (also called self-containment) is the state of not requiring any aid, support, or interaction, for survival; it is therefore a type of personal or collective autonomy. On a national scale, a totally self-sufficient economy that does not trade with the outside world is called an autarky.

"The term self-sufficiency is usually applied to varieties of sustainable living in which nothing is consumed outside of what is produced by the self-sufficient individuals. Examples of attempts at self-sufficiency in North America include simple living, homesteading, off-the-grid, survivalism, DIY ethic and the back-to-the-land movement.

"Practices that enable or aid self-sufficiency include autonomous building, permaculture, sustainable agriculture, and renewable energy.

"The term is also applied to limited forms of self-sufficiency, for example growing one's own food or becoming economically independent of state subsidies.

"The entire population of the world was, at one time, self-sufficient. They made their own clothing, tools, weapons, boats, huts, and food. They used gathering, hunting, herding and farming to find/hunt/grow their own food. As the human population of the world grew, the wild food supply dwindled. People began to rely on herding and farming more; relying less upon gathering and hunting. In modern times, automated food production on farms makes food. The vast populations now depend on a few farmers to make their food for them. Many in developed nations now depend on job salaries to buy food, clothes, and shelter, rather than making these things from raw materials found in the environment. But in a few places in the world, native societies continue to be self-sufficient, never having given up their traditional ways of food gathering and food making. Because these native peoples have no jobs and make no salaries, they are often listed as unemployed."

Sustainability's definition according to Wikipedia is: "a lifestyle that attempts to reduce an individual's or society's use of the Earth's natural resources and personal resources. Practitioners of sustainable living often attempt to reduce their carbon footprint by altering methods of transportation, energy consumption, and diet. Proponents of sustainable living aim to conduct their lives in ways that are consistent with sustainability, in natural balance and respectful of humanity's symbiotic relationship with the Earth's natural ecology and cycles. The practice and general philosophy of ecological living is highly interrelated with the overall principles of sustainable development."

Sustainability seeks to not only incorporate every aspect of natural living & resources into a smooth arrangement of small-scale production, but also tries to use up every last item, product & byproduct so there is little to no waste, & it can naturally sustain itself in that cycle. For example, having goats not only gives milk most of the year for fresh goat milk & a variety of homemade cheeses & dairy products, but also with many varieties you can spin the hair just like wool into textiles, & the manure & such from cleaning out the pen goes automatically to compost, & also is naturally clean enough to be sprinkled directly into the garden. Ever-nibbling goats can also be used to clean out many natural weeds & underbrush that grows thickly, assisting in clearing land that needs de-brushed & in return, enriching their milk supply & quality with fresh live plants & herbs.

The list can go on, & on. Sustainability can even be as simple and thoughtful as the practice of saving roast chicken & other meat carcasses from one meal, to boil into nourishing bone broths for soup, and make an entire second meal from the scraps instead of tossing them. The various Native American tribes are one of the most perfect examples of complete sustainability I can think of, where literally nothing went to waste & everything, even sinews/tendons from the deer carcass had a purpose (sewing thread), & even the deer's brains were used to tan the raw pelts/skin into soft leather for their moccasins.

I encourage you to have a playful spirit while dabbling in all of this & getting your feet wet... if something goes awry, it generally isn't the end of the world (although it might seem so at the time, i.e. if the goats get out again & try trampling what's left of the garden... that they *didn't* already nibble on for their lunch buffet!) & will be the source of a good belly laugh or two later. Many things will take practice & skill, and still more will be very easy. The process is just as large a part as the end result.

# Chapter 2: Different Types of Gardens, & Tips On Incorporating Permaculture & Bio dynamics Into the Landscape

Organic Gardening, first of all, is the approach I advocate for many reasons. It is by far the most wholesome, holistic way, and the closest to Nature. There are literally hundreds of books written on the subject, & I encourage you to check out Mother Earth News magazine, blogs & all of their massive online resources (as well as any other seemingly useful books & resources you come across in your search) to learn nearly everything, from the very basics of organic gardening & farming, to advanced techniques, garden plans, homestead plans, & thousands of other amazing correlating topics. Organic gardening does not use chemicals, pesticides, or insecticides whatsoever, as well as utilizing zero GMO seeds/products(genetically modified organisms), all of which have been shown in study after study to be very harmful to our health, and contraindicative of getting back to the land & healing nature & each other. Organic gardening instead incorporates useful, creative ways to control "weed" & insect/pest populations through companion planting, hand methods, natural fertilizers, & more.

Permaculture is, according to Wiki, "A branch of ecological design, ecological engineering, environmental design, construction and Integrated Water Resources Management that develops sustainable architecture, regenerative and self-maintained habitat and agricultural systems modeled from natural ecosystems. The term permaculture (as a systematic method) was first coined by Australians Bill Mollison and David Holmgren in 1978. The word permaculture originally referred to "permanent agriculture" but was expanded to stand also for "permanent culture," as it was seen that social aspects were integral to a truly sustainable system as inspired by Masanobu Fukuoka's natural farming philosophy.

"Permaculture is a philosophy of working with, rather than against nature; of protracted and thoughtful observation rather than protracted and thoughtless labor; and of looking at plants and animals in all their functions, rather than treating any area as a single product system." - Bill Mollison

The Core Tenets of Permaculture are as follows:

Care for the earth: Provision for all life systems to continue and multiply. This is the first principle, because without a healthy earth, humans cannot flourish.

Care for the people: Provision for people to access those resources necessary for their existence.

Return of surplus: Reinvesting surpluses back into the system to provide for the first two ethics. This includes returning waste back into the system to recycle into usefulness.

Permaculture design emphasizes patterns of landscape, function, and species assemblies. It determines where these elements should be placed so they can provide maximum benefit to the local environment. The central concept of permaculture is maximizing useful connections between components and synergy of the final design. The focus of permaculture, therefore, is not on each separate element, but rather on the relationships created among elements by the way they are placed together; the whole becoming greater than the sum of its parts. Permaculture design therefore seeks to minimize waste, human labor, and energy input by building systems with maximal benefits between design elements to achieve a high level of synergy. Permaculture designs evolve over time by taking into account these relationships and elements and can become extremely complex systems that produce a high density of food and materials with minimal input.

The design principles which are the conceptual foundation of permaculture were derived from the science of systems ecology and study of pre-industrial examples of sustainable land use. Permaculture draws from several disciplines including organic farming, agroforestry, integrated farming, sustainable development, and applied ecology. Permaculture has been applied most commonly to the design of housing and landscaping, integrating techniques such as agroforestry, natural building, and rainwater harvesting within the context of permaculture design principles and theory.

Observe and interact: By taking time to engage with nature we can design solutions that suit our particular situation.

Catch and store energy: By developing systems that collect resources at peak abundance, we can use them in times of need.

Obtain a yield: Ensure that you are getting truly useful rewards as part of the work that you are doing.

Apply self-regulation and accept feedback: We need to discourage inappropriate activity to ensure that systems can continue to function well.

Use and value renewable resources and services: Make the best use of nature's abundance to reduce our consumptive behavior and dependence on non-renewable resources.

Produce no waste: By valuing and making use of all the resources that are available to us, nothing goes to waste.

Design from patterns to details: By stepping back, we can observe patterns in nature and society. These can form the backbone of our designs, with the details filled in as we go.

Integrate rather than segregate: By putting the right things in the right place, relationships develop between those things and they work together to support each other.

Use small and slow solutions: Small and slow systems are easier to maintain than big ones, making better use of local resources and producing more sustainable outcomes.

Use and value diversity: Diversity reduces vulnerability to a variety of threats and takes advantage of the unique nature of the environment in which it resides.

Use edges and value the marginal: The interface between things is where the most interesting events take place. These are often the most valuable, diverse and productive elements in the system.

Creatively use and respond to change: We can have a positive impact on inevitable change by carefully observing, and then intervening at the right time.


LAYERS are one of the tools used to design functional ecosystems that are both sustainable and of direct benefit to humans. A mature ecosystem has a huge number of relationships between its component parts: trees, understory, ground cover, soil, fungi, insects, and animals. Because plants grow to different heights, a diverse community of life is able to grow in a relatively small space, as each layer is stacked one on top of another. There are generally seven recognized layers in a food forest, although some practitioners also include fungi as an eighth layer & from my own experience, they are definitely worth adding to the list!


The canopy: the tallest trees in the system. Large trees dominate but typically do not saturate the area, i.e. there exist patches barren of trees.

Understory layer: trees that revel in the dappled light under the canopy.

Shrubs: a diverse layer of woody perennials of limited height. includes most berry bushes.

Herbaceous: Plants in this layer die back to the ground every winter (if winters are cold enough, that is). They do not produce woody stems as the Shrub layer does. Many culinary and medicinal herbs are in this layer. A large variety of beneficial plants fall into this layer. May be annuals, biennials or perennials

Soil surface/Groundcover: There is some overlap with the Herbaceous layer and the Groundcover layer; however plants in this layer grow much closer to the ground, grow densely to fill bare patches of soil, and often can tolerate some foot traffic. cover crops retain soil and lessen erosion, along with green manures that add nutrients and organic matter to the soil, especially nitrogen

Rhizosphere: Root layers within the soil. The major components of this layer are the soil and the organisms that live within it such as plant roots (including root crops such as potatoes and other edible tubers), fungi, insects, nematodes, worms, etc.

Vertical layer: climbers or vines, such as runner beans and lima beans (vine varieties)."

There are many incredible additional resources online including pre-made plans & "cheatsheets" of already carefully-thought-out permaculture landscape designs, especially for the Temperate Regions of North America & the United Kingdom. I encourage you as always to look into all of this deeply, & choose for yourself & family what would work for you, with the amount & type of land you live upon, etcetera. Imagine incorporating free-range animals like farm fowl as well into the landscape, to pick bugs (chickens, guinea fowl, geese, turkeys, Cornish game hens, ducks etc.), manure the soil naturally, move topsoil & scratch it up, etc... it is wonderful to put into place and then watch it all come together!

BIODYNAMIC Farming is a holistic approach to agriculture, taking "organic" to a much higher level, and experiencing a remarkable growth of interest in recent years with the advent of the modern Homesteading movement. It is worth an enormous looking into & incorporating into your garden designing, plans & education.

According to Dark Rye, an online magazine, "Biodynamic agriculture is designed to restore the integrity of the natural environment and enhance the quality and health of food.

Biodynamic farmers manage their farms—including fields, woods, wetlands, plants, animals and people—as an interconnected whole, full of dignity and life. Each farm thus takes on the character of an "individuality" that reflects the unique qualities of a particular place, climate and community. This ecological, ethical and spiritual stewardship of the earth produces food with extraordinary flavor, quality and nutrition.

Biodynamics was developed in central Europe in the early 1920s by the Austrian philosopher and social reformer Rudolf Steiner; it is now practiced on more than 350,000 acres of farmland in 47 countries. Steiner was one of the pioneers of the organic farming movement, and biodynamics is considered by many to be the most advanced and holistic form of organic farming and gardening on the planet. Steiner's insights have also led to innovative movements in a number of other fields such as education (Waldorf Schools), medicine, finance and social therapy.

Steiner developed biodynamics in partnership with a group of farmers who were concerned with the decline in soil and animal health that they were witnessing on their farms. This was just at the time when a highly mechanistic view of nature was beginning to take hold in agriculture, which led to the development and use of synthetically produced nitrogen fertilizers. Steiner was one of the first public figures to warn that the widespread use of chemical fertilizers would lead to the decline of soil, plant and animal health and the subsequent devitalization of food.

Biodynamics came to North America in the early 1930s, and over the past 75 years, its practitioners have played a key role in the renewal of agriculture here, helping pioneer the early organic farming movement; inspiring the work of Silent Spring author Rachel Carson; and starting the first community-supported agriculture (CSA) programs. Founded in 1938, the Biodynamic Association supports this growing and vital movement through conferences, a journal, farmer training and research.

Biodynamics is based on a view of nature as a living, self-sustaining organism that unites material, biological and spiritual elements. Biodynamic methods are designed to stimulate and sustain the farm's inherent fertility and health through the integration of crops and livestock, the restoration of on-farm biodiversity, and thoughtful cooperation with the influences of the sun, moon and planets on the earth.

Biodynamic farmers strive to find a balance and diversity of crops and livestock that enables the farm to be as self-sustaining as possible. Animals are stocked at a rate so that their manure provides adequate fertility for the crops being grown, and sufficient acreage is devoted to pasture and forage to provide for the needs of the animals. Thus, imported fertilizers and feeds are kept to a minimum, and this contributes both to the ecological health of the farm and the development of a true farm "individuality" that is a coherent whole.

Biodynamics also incorporates the use of nine preparations made from fermented manure, herbs (yarrow, chamomile, stinging nettle, oak bark, dandelion, valerian and horsetail) and the mineral silica. The biodynamic preparations are used as field sprays and in the making of compost to stimulate specific health-giving processes within the farm. The preparations enhance the beneficial effects of good farming practices and have been shown to help remediate the impact of pollution and balance the effects of extreme weather.

Another unique aspect of biodynamic agriculture is the attention paid to the influences and rhythms of the sun, moon and planets.

Just as the moon creates the tides in our oceans, each of these celestial bodies has subtle influences on the growth and development of plants and animals. Based on Steiner's insights and subsequent research, a number of biodynamic calendars have been developed that offer indications for optimal times for sowing, cultivating and harvesting, based on the cyclical changes in the positions of the celestial bodies in relation to the earth.

Biodynamics is ultimately not just a set of alternative agricultural methods but a new way of seeing and understanding the natural world. Steiner called for and pioneered a new form of science—which he called spiritual science—that could grapple with both the material and nonmaterial or spiritual aspects of reality. Biodynamic farmers work to develop their capacity to sense and observe the more subtle forces at work in nature, and to use their own insights to further enhance the vitality of their farms. The biodynamic methods are thus in a continuous state of evolution and individualization.

As part of his work on a new approach to science, Steiner also developed, together with a number of colleagues, a set of unique, scientific methods for demonstrating the presence of life forces in nature and for evaluating the quality and vitality of food and soil. These methods, sometimes called the "picture-forming methods," are finding growing acceptance in scientific circles in Europe. These and other traditional forms of scientific research have consistently demonstrated the benefits of biodynamic methods.

Most biodynamic farms also seek to embody innovative approaches to the economic dimension of the farm, taking inspiration from Steiner's insights into social and economic life that emphasized the need for cooperation and transparency. The aim to create associative economic relationships between farms and consumers sparked the CSA movement, which originated with biodynamic farms and has now been taken up by more than 6,000 farms in the United States. Many biodynamic practitioners also work in creative partnerships with other farms and with schools, medical and wellness facilities, restaurants, hotels, homes for social therapy and other community-based organizations.

Biodynamics has an independent certification system managed worldwide by Demeter International and in the United States by Demeter USA.

Demeter certification in this country uses the USDA organic standards as a foundation but goes beyond them in several important ways. For example, the Demeter Biodynamic® Farm Standard requires the healthy integration of crops and livestock on the farm, as well as a certain amount of wild or uncultivated land as part of its biodiversity requirement. It also requires use of the biodynamic preparations described above. In addition, whereas organic certification can be applied to just one part of a farm, Demeter certification must encompass the whole farm.3

To counter the growing depletion of the vitality of our food, farms and communities by the modern industrial agricultural system, we need more than an alternative lifestyle movement. We need more than anti-GMO activism, and more than a big toolbox of alternative farming techniques. We need a revolutionary new way of understanding nature and the role of agriculture in the life of society. We need deep medicine for the land, for our communities and for ourselves. Biodynamics offers a pathway into deep agricultural renewal. It is a way of seeing, a way of farming, and a way of creating community that restores the very heart of what it means to be human on Earth.

For more information about biodynamics and how you can get involved, please contact the Biodynamic Association at www.biodynamics.com."

Agroforestry

Forest Gardening, Forest Permaculture, or Agroforestry, ties in closely with overall homesteading permaculture as well, in wondrous ways for your homestead. Wikipedia's definition of "Forest Gardening" is as follows:

"Forest gardening is a low-maintenance sustainable plant-based food production and agroforestry system based on woodland ecosystems, incorporating fruit and nut trees, shrubs, herbs, vines and perennial vegetables which have yields directly useful to humans. Making use of companion planting, these can be intermixed to grow in a succession of layers, to build a woodland habitat.

Forest gardening is a prehistoric method of securing food in tropical areas. In the 1980s, Robert Hart coined the term "forest gardening" after adapting the principles and applying them to temperate climates.

Forest gardens are probably the world's oldest form of land use and most resilient agro ecosystem. They originated in prehistoric times along jungle-clad river banks and in the wet foothills of monsoon regions. In the gradual process of families improving their immediate environment, useful tree and vine species were identified, protected and improved whilst undesirable species were eliminated. Eventually superior foreign species were selected and incorporated into the gardens.

Forest gardens are still common in the tropics and known by various names such as: home gardens in Kerala in South India, Nepal, Zambia, Zimbabwe and Tanzania; Kandyan forest gardens in Sri Lanka; huertos familiares, the "family orchards" of Mexico; and pekarangan, the gardens of "complete design", in Java. These are also called agroforests and, where the wood components are short-statured, the term shrub garden is employed. Forest gardens have been shown to be a significant source of income and food security for local populations.

*The Seven Layers of the Forest Garden*

Robert Hart pioneered a system based on the observation that the natural forest can be divided into distinct levels. He used intercropping to develop an existing small orchard of apples and pears into an edible polyculture landscape consisting of the following layers:

'Canopy layer' consisting of the original mature fruit trees.

'Low-tree layer' of smaller nut and fruit trees on dwarfing root stocks.

'Shrub layer' of fruit bushes such as currants and berries.

'Herbaceous layer' of perennial vegetables and herbs.

'Rhizosphere' or 'underground' dimension of plants grown for their roots and tubers.

'Ground cover layer' of edible plants that spread horizontally.

'Vertical layer' of vines and climbers.

A key component of the seven-layer system was the plants he selected. Most of the traditional vegetable crops grown today, such as carrots, are sun loving plants not well selected for the more shady forest garden system. Hart favored shade tolerant perennial vegetables.

Robert Hart adapted forest gardening for the United Kingdom's temperate climate during the 1980s. His theories were later developed by Martin Crawford from the Agroforestry Research Trust and various permaculturalists such as Graham Bell, Patrick Whitefield, Dave Jacke and Geoff Lawton."

Going back to & examining all of recorded history, which we now are gifted to be able to research & learn from via careful use of modern technology, are seriously all worth looking into... Study everything you can find that piques your interest. Create fusions of techniques & skills. Keep a permaculturing journal as you go along, maps of plants, & lists of their uses. Teach others & learn how to use every last edible plant & herb, try growing a little of everything you could ever think of needing, as a fun hobby, and watch it blossom into beautiful self-sustainability. Trade/barter with other gardeners & permaculture gardeners, for homemade fertilizers, manure concoctions, plants, herbs & even animals/fowl you need- swapping plant/tree cuttings with one another is a fun pastime, for instance- & you both shall be enriched in turn. Find edible native plants that grow in your area with little to no effort & incorporate this vast reserve, species by species, into your own homestead permaculture landscape.

# Chapter 3: Preserving Food; Making Bread, Butter and Cheese

Once you have your gardens planted & thriving, Organic Permaculture & Biodynamic Edible Landscaping started, & everything is glowing & growing just as divine & fresh with each new dawn as Eden must have, then the question comes: how do I harvest all this & what's more, preserve all these things?? And to top it all off, how do I create a hearty loaf of bread with fresh homemade raw butter, & a creamy delicious cheese to complement all of this, my beautiful, sacred, life-giving organic bounty??

First of all, there are a variety of ways to preserve your precious cornucopia. Dehydrating/drying; preserving in oils & vinegars, syrups, jams & alcohols; canning, freezing, pickling, fermenting; packing root cellars, and more. Many foods can be preserved in a variety of ways, while others lend themselves to one certain particular way best. I will provide an overview of each of the methods I have mentioned, and of course encourage you once more to research each foodstuff closely to see what you can do, & above all play & experiment!!! Have fun with it as much as you can, try new dishes & preserve those or just preserve the raw ingredients as you would get them from the store (i.e. frozen corn kernels, dried basil, pickled cucumbers, etcetera). The sky is the limit & with the internet now at our fingertips, we have a unique opportunity others before us didn't have: we can borrow from ALL cultures now & research all their traditional recipes, ways, tips & tricks like never before, creating new dishes, products & fusions previously unthought-of!

Dehydration is simply a fancy word for drying. There is the traditional methods such as laying them out on a blanket in the sun to dry for several days/weeks (like grapes into raisins, & plums into prunes). There is the easy way to bundle herbs & greens in bunches & hang them to dry to flavor winter soups & stews, which doubles as a very attractive, homey, old-fashioned decorating touch to boot! Then there is the relatively new item, the dehydrator, which tends to dry things more evenly, quickly & still maintain the raw enzymes of foods, which is ultimately best. The "Excalibur" dehydrator is by far a modern homesteading classic, with a square shape & lots of room for tray inserts to make homemade fruit leather & such. The downside is that they are also significantly pricey usually. There are many other smaller rounded electric dehydrators that are easily purchased for less, and my friend personally has the best of luck finding the round ones at thrift stores & passing them on, she gave me three of them that way & I absolutely love them!!! If you choose to go the non-electric route & are feeling adventurous, I believe you can find plans to make your own solar-powered, nonelectric dehydrator online even. I encourage you to find the method that works best for what you want to do, on any scale.

Many herbs & flowers can be preserved for months or even years by properly preserving in oils, vinegar, alcohol, or simple sugar syrups. Research each method & don't be afraid to try little aromatic combinations you think would be beautiful! For example, fresh or dried herbs in olive oil is a classic! Make sure they are clean & unblemished & there isn't an ounce of spare moisture first. Pat them with towels or blot with paper towels or cloth napkins, pack them into a glass jar or tall slim bottle with a cork, fill with olive oil or any oil you wish to try, add salt, pepper & spices if you'd like even. Cover & let sit out of direct sunlight for several weeks to several months, checking occasionally. You can use this oil in salad dressings, in cooking, drizzled as a special garnish, & more. Vinegar is used much the same way- try a good high-quality vinegar like Bragg's apple cider vinegar, and others like red wine vinegar or even plain white vinegar if you'd like. Each gives a different taste & lends its unique characteristics to different uses.

The same goes for preserving things in alcohols like brandy or vodka, etc., (Try packing cacao nibs, or fresh blackberries for starters, in brandy!! Check occasionally on the progress- the former takes a month or two to flavor it, the latter anywhere from 6 months to a year- and believe me, it is worth it!!) And simple sugar syrups which are similar to preserves only without the pectin to make it gel into a jelly or jam... they are very simple indeed! I generally preserve roses in a simple sugar syrup, & they are just beautiful & delightfully delicious that way used sparingly on things as a garnish- what a treat! Rose petal jam is used in Ayurveda to soothe & cool the body & is a good daily tonic for women, take a teaspoon a day & put it on toast, in tea, etc. How I make it )or any other simple syrup too) generally, is I simmer a few handfuls of rose petals (fresh or dried) into water to make a rose tea, then either strain it or leave them in, they are beautiful no matter what the color. I then start adding sugar (You can use raw organic sugar if you'd like) & dissolve several cup-fulls into the mix, taking care to turn the heat down & keep a close eye so it doesn't burn. Once it all has dissolved, take it off the heat & let it cool. I love making rhubarb simple syrup this way too & pouring it over vanilla bean ice-cream for an amazing treat after a hot summer day. Hibiscus flowers are incredible this way too, although it is advisable to strain the flowers before bottling. I also make a hot ginger concentrate syrup this way, to use in tea, alcoholic mixed drinks, & etcetera. Experiment!

Canning, a method of first sterilizing glass jars & then filling them with whatever you wish, is a time-consuming & particular method of food preservation which is also worth every ounce of the process, because once the food is canned & cooled & hermetically sealed, it requires no more energy to store for at least a year. There are two methods of canning: Water bath canning & Pressure canning. The former uses a large water bath canner rather like an oversized soup pot with a little cage inside to hold the jars still, and heated to boiling to properly process & activate the seal. This method is best for many things such as canned fruits & vegetables, jams, jellies, preserves, pickles, krauts, & more. Pressure canning uses a pressure canner rather like a pressure cooker to sterilize & put the contents under high pressure, which is good for different things such as canning meats, soups & heavier things, dry bean mixes even, & more. Each has amazing purpose & use in food preservation with the same end result: rows of freshly-canned jars of food lined up to store & feast upon for a long, cold winter anywhere.

Freezer-preserving, although still needing electricity in most climates to keep the food continuously frozen until consumed, is one of my personal favorites to preserve all manner of things swiftly & effectively. From chopped, tenuous fresh herbs like chives & garlic scapes, to fully prepared meals, and everything in-between including sauces, fresh juices, even jams & everything liquid or solid, you can easily freezer-preserve all of the above by using heavy zip lock freezer bags, filling half-way, making sure no air remains in the other half of the bag before sealing, and then lying flat in the freezer to freeze in a perfect square before removing them & stacking them upright across in perfect, labeled stacks- it is so satisfying! You will never want for a quick meal if you make a little extra soup, sauce etc. & freeze some right away like this. I like to joke that freezer-preserved meals is equivalent to homegrown, organic fast-food- just take it out, thaw & reheat! Healthy & delicious.

Pickling is another wonderful, fun & effective method of preservation, the most common being the classic picked cucumbers, although almost any vegetable as well as a variety of other produce may be preserved by pickling as well. Try carrot pickles, one of my family's favorites! You can actually store pickles in a cool, dark place like a dark pantry or root cellar below ground, in a barrel or large jars, for several months. Refrigeration is generally more common these days in America, but not required right away at least. If you want to extend them longer/indefinitely, then merely can them in pint or quart jars in a water bath canner- pickles can pretty easily. You can try pickling by buying a little kit or mix which is very easy, Ball Canning Co. makes them as well as others, or you can prepare your own pickling mix from scratch. I will provide a recipe here for you to adapt to whatever you would like to try pickling, here is a beautiful & delightful mixture for you to try:

Blanch 1/3 pound each halved baby carrots, green beans and yellow beans, 2 to 4 minutes. Cool in ice water, then put in a glass bowl with 1/2 sliced red onion. Make the brine: Boil 2 cups each white vinegar and water, 1/4 cup kosher salt, 2 bay leaves, 3/4 cup sugar, the zest and juice of 1 lemon, and 1 teaspoon each peppercorns and coriander seeds; I also add plenty of fresh garlic pieces, whole or chopped. Pour over the vegetables, then let cool. Chill at least 4 hours.

\*\*\*

Fermentation as both a method of preserving, & a healthy lifestyle choice, is so special I have devoted an entire chapter to help you get started (See Chapter 5: Introduction To Probiotic Fermentation for details), so we will pass over it here for now.

BREAD-baking is wholeheartedly satisfying of an activity, as well as an age-old one. There are obviously many kinds of breads you can make depending on what you love to eat & pair with your meals: Artisan hearth breads are really worth trying, although they are only briefly covered here below. There is an entire art to making a perfect baguette/crusty loaf of shatter-crisp-crusted bread with a soft, velvety center, & it's also the perfect showcase for homemade butter slathered on top or, the foundation for a *perfect* bruschetta. I have included a basic, classic Greek Peasant Country Loaf recipe similar to French, Italian & any rustic artisan breads..... As well as the more primitive & ancient unleavened chapati, the Indian/Far Eastern flatbreads similar to the pitas of the Middle East.

Here are my top two favorite bread recipes:

*Delicious, Easy Indian Flatbreads/Chapatis*

Ingredients

2 cups whole wheat flour, plus more for rolling

Big pinch fine sea salt

1 cup water

1/4 cup olive oil, vegetable oil, melted butter, or ghee

Directions

Pour the flour and salt into a large bowl. Slowly pour water into the flour, moving your other hand through the flour in circular motions, until it starts to come together. Then, either in the bowl or on your counter (which you might want to lightly flour to prevent sticking), knead the dough for about 10 minutes. The dough should be soft and pliant.

Return the ball of dough to the bowl and rub the surface of the dough with a little oil to keep it from drying out. Cover with plastic wrap or a damp cloth and allow to rest about 30 minutes.

When you're ready to make chapatis, assemble your tools: a small, flat bowl of whole wheat flour, a small bowl of olive oil or melted butter with a small spoon in it, and a paper towel-lined plate or container for the finished breads.

Heat a flat griddle or cast iron skillet over medium-high heat. Meanwhile, on a lightly-floured surface, work the ball of dough into a long log. Cut into 12 equal pieces by cutting it in half, and then half again. Cut each of the quarters into 3 equal pieces. Return to the bowl and cover with a damp towel to prevent them from drying out.

To roll the chapatis: Roll a piece of dough between your palms to form a ball, and then flatten with your palm. Dunk this puck in the bowl of flour, and then roll until it's a 4-inch circle. Spoon about 1/4 teaspoon of oil in the center of the circle, and spread it out almost to the perimeter of the circle using the back of the spoon. Fold the circle in half, then in half again, so it forms a triangle. Seal the edges, and dunk in flour again if it's sticky.

Start rolling, turning the triangle a quarter turn after each roll, until it's about 6-inches wide, with an even thickness. After some practice you'll be able to roll the chapati and rotate it without picking it up; I do this by weighing down a little on my right hand and pushing the chapati around that way.

Test the griddle by sprinkling a little flour on it; if it turns brown immediately, it's ready. Flapping the chapati between your hands to remove any excess flour, slap the chapati onto the griddle. It should start darkening almost immediately.

When small bubbles start to form, spread a little oil over the surface of the chapati, then flip. It should start to puff up. Spoon a little oil over this side too, and when it's puffed up a little more, flip. Press down on the edges of the chapati with your spatula or (if you're brave!) with a dry rag. This will seal the edges and encourage the entire chapati to puff up. If you spot any holes, press down on those too so the air doesn't escape. Allowing the air to stay inside the whole chapati makes it flaky and light. But don't fret if your first few don't puff up; it takes practice! It will still taste utterly delicious.

Remove to your container. Repeat with the remaining dough, and serve the chapatis hot.

\*\*\*

*Classic Greek Country Bread* (Can easily be made with Fermented Sourdough Starter, covered later in the Fermentation chapter)

In villages around Greece, this classic bread is still baked in outdoor wood-burning ovens. This bread is denser than other types of bread (the loaf at right measures about 13 inches across and weighs a little more than 2 pounds) and can be made with a variety of flours or a combination of more than one. If you have your own sourdough starter, use 1/2 pound (slightly less than one cup for most starters) in place of the yeast in the recipe.

Prep Time: 3 hours, 20 minutes

Cook Time: 30 minutes

Total Time: 3 hours, 50 minutes

Ingredients:

1 ounce of fresh yeast or 2 tablespoons of dry yeast

1/2 cup (4 fl.oz) of lukewarm water

1/2 cup (62g) of flour (whatever type used for bread)

2 1/5 pounds (1 kilo / 8 cups) of bread flour (whole wheat, barley, white, corn, or other)

1 tablespoon of salt

2 1/2 cups (20 fl.oz) of lukewarm water

2 tablespoons of milk

2 tablespoons of olive oil

2 tablespoons of honey


Preparation:


In a small bowl, dissolve the yeast in lukewarm water. Slowly add the 1/2 cup of flour and mix until all lumps of flour have dissolved, to form a thick liquid. Allow to rise about 15-20 minutes.


Note: If using sourdough starter, omit this step, and make a sponge with 1/2 pound of starter, the 1/2 cup of lukewarm water, and 1/2 cup of flour. Set aside to rise for 2 hours.

Sift the remaining flour with the salt, put in a large mixing bowl, and make a well in the center. Add oil, honey, milk, yeast mixture (or sourdough starter), and 2 cups of the water in the well. Pulling in the flour slowly, mix with hands until it's a cohesive mass. (If more water is needed, add in small amounts from the remaining 1/2 cup.) Turn out onto a floured surface and continue kneading until the dough is nice and smooth and no longer sticks to the hands.


Place the dough in a lightly oiled mixing bowl and roll until all sides of the dough are lightly oiled. Cover the bowl with 3 dishtowels: one dry, one dampened with warm water (wet towel and wring out), and the other dry. Place in a warm place and allow to rise until doubled, about 1 1/2 to 2 hours.


Punch down and knead for 5-6 minutes on a floured surface. Divide the dough into the number of loaves you want to make (this works well in 3-4 loaves), and form into round or oblong or baguette shaped loaves. Place several inches apart on ungreased cookie sheets and cover with 3 clean dishtowels (the middle one damp). In a warm place, allow the loaves to rise for 1 hour.

Preheat oven to 450F (220C).

For a thicker crust, score the tops of the loaves in 3 or 4 places (see photo). Otherwise, bake as is on the rack just below the middle of the oven for 30-35 minutes until browned. When tapped on the bottom, bread will sound hollow.

When the loaves are done, remove from oven and cool on racks.

Notes:

Use a good "strong" flour - i.e., hard flour, also known as bread flour.

If the honey you're using is very thick, place the jar in a saucepan containing 1 inch of water and warm.

No honey on hand, or don't care for it? Leave it out.

***

*How To Make Butter, and Cultured Butter*

~Makes about 1 cup of butter and 8 ounces of buttermilk~

If you've never tried cultured butter — the more sophisticated, deeply-flavored version of butter — then you simply must try it!

What You Need

Ingredients

1 pint (2 cups) heavy cream, preferably organic and not ultra-pasturized

2 tablespoons plain yogurt (optional)

Scant 1/4 teaspoon of salt (optional)

2 or 3 cups of ice water, for washing the butter


Equipment


Optional culturing equipment:

Bowl

Measuring cups and spoons

Whisk

Clean kitchen cloth


To make the butter:

Sturdy sieve

Cheesecloth or clean napkin

Bowl for catching buttermilk

Stand mixer, hand mixer, food processor, or canning jar (or other covered container)

Plastic wrap or kitchen cloth

Spatula or wooden spoon

Clean containers for butter and buttermilk

Waxed paper or parchment paper (optional)

Instructions

Culture the cream (optional): The day before you would like to make your butter, pour the cream into a bowl (I like to use the bowl of my stand mixer) and add the yogurt. Whisk briefly to combine and cover the bowl with a clean kitchen towel. Set in a slightly warm place (about 70°F - 75°F) to culture. Check after 8 to 12 hours. The cream is ready when it has thickened slightly and is a little foamy. It will smell slightly sour and tangy. This can possibly take an additional 12 to 24 (see Recipe Notes). Once it has cultured, place it in the refrigerator for about 1 hour to chill. → If you did not culture your butter, let it warm on the counter for about an hour (to about 60°F) before churning.

Prepare the sieve and mixer: Place a sturdy sieve over a bowl and line with a few layers of cheesecloth or a clean napkin. You can use a stand mixer, a hand mixer, a food processor, or a canning jar to churn your cream. (See Recipe Notes below if you want use a canning jar.)

Prepare the cream and mixer for churning: Place the cream in the bowl of your mixer or processor. Cover the top with plastic wrap or a kitchen towel to prevent splattering.

Churn the cream: Turn on the mixer to medium-high. The cream will first whip into peaks (at around 2 minutes) and then become grainy (around 3 minutes). Keep whipping until the solid mass (butter) and liquid (buttermilk) are separated (about 5 minutes total). The mixture will splatter heavily in the final stages of churning, so be sure the plastic wrap is secure. The process may take a little longer, up to 8 to 10 minutes, although it usually takes me less than 5 minutes.

Strain off the buttermilk: Pour the buttermilk through the cheesecloth and strainer, holding the butter solid back. Allow the buttermilk to strain through, then plop in the butter. Gather the cloth around the butter and press it hard with your fist. Do this several times to get as much buttermilk out of the butter as possible. Pour the buttermilk into a container, label and refrigerate.

Wash the butter: Rinse out the bowl used for buttermilk. Remove the butter from the cloth and place it in the bowl. Add 1/2 cup of ice water to the bowl, and using a spatula, press the butter into the ice water. It will quickly become cloudy with buttermilk. Pour off the cloudy water, add another 1/2 cup of ice water to the bowl, and keep pressing. Repeat until the water is clear. This may take up to 6 washings. The butter will firm up towards the end, so you may find it easier to use your hands.

Salt the butter (optional): Sprinkle the salt over the butter and knead in. Again, your hands may be the best tool here.

Store the butter. Pack the butter into a jar with a cover, or roll it into a log using waxed paper or parchment paper. The butter will keep in the refrigerator for about three weeks or can be frozen for several months.

*Recipe Notes

Culturing the Cream:

Culturing the cream before you churn it is really the way to go, in my opinion. You don't have to do this to make good butter, but you do have to do it to make great butter! Transcendent butter! Back before refrigeration, all butter was cultured as a way to keep it from spoiling. It's super easy to do, but you do need to allow for some extra time for the culturing (usually 12 to 24 hours), so you can skip this step if time is not on your side.

There are butter cultures you can purchase from cheese-making suppliers, but I simply use yogurt since it is so readily available. Try to avoid an overly processed yogurt. My yogurt contains milk and yogurt culture and nothing else — no stabilizers, flavorings, or other additives. Homemade live-culture yogurt is best!

Additional notes on culturing: Many factors will influence how long the cream takes to culture: ambient room temperature, how your cream was processed and pasteurized, how your yogurt was processed and pasteurized, etc. If the cream cultures too quickly and you're not ready to make the butter yet, simply put it into the refrigerator until you are ready. Just be sure you remove it about an hour before churning so that it can warm up a bit. Cultured cream will be thickened and slightly foamy, and it will have a somewhat tangy, almost yogurt-like smell. Trust your senses! If you feel it is too strong and has gone bad, just throw it away. But remember that the yogurt is introducing beneficial cultures that help prevent spoilage, so the likelihood of this happening is small.

Unplugged butter: You can skip the electric mixer/processor and simply shake your cream in a covered canning jar or well-sealed container until it forms into the butter mass. This can take a while, up to 20 minutes or more, so be prepared for a work-out or solicit some help.

Culturing Temperatures

The cream will need to sit at a slightly warm temperature to culture, about 70°F to 75°F. Once it's cultured, it should be chilled to about 60°F to churn properly. Personally, I never measure temperatures when I make butter: after culturing, I pop the bowl into the refrigerator for about 1 hour to chill it. If I don't think I will churn it right away, I leave it in the fridge for longer and then let it rest at room temperature for about an hour to take some of the chill off.


What about Salt?

Since I use my home-churned butter for spreading and cooking, a little salt is a nice addition. It improves the flavor and contributes to its shelf life as salt is a natural preservative. But it is optional and if you're not sure how you will be using your butter, you may want to leave it out. If you do add salt, be sure to add it at the very end so you don't rinse it away in the final washing process.


What's With the Washing?

Even after the butter has been drained and pressed, it's still holding onto a lot of buttermilk. You want to rinse out as much of this as possible as the buttermilk will contribute to early spoilage. Some people like to squeeze the butter in their hands under cold running water, but I prefer the ice water in a bowl method (see recipe).

Recipe can easily be doubled.

\*\*\*


HOMEMADE CHEESE

*Easy Chevre: A Perfect Beginner's Soft Cheese*


Don't be intimidated by the cheese making process, I promise you this is one of the easiest cheese recipes you will ever find!


You will need only 4 ingredients: 1 gallon of goat milk (you can half this recipe), rennet (you can use the junket tablets or a liquid), a culture or dash of lemon juice, and 1/4 cup of water. Some people use a double strength vegetable rennet... a little goes a long way! You can make chevre with pasteurized goat milk but if you have access to fresh raw milk of either goat or cow, the flavor tends to be more complex and buttery. Okay, are you ready for this? Pour your milk into a large container, I used my crock pot because I do not like to use metal. If you must use metal make sure it is stainless steel so it will be non-reactive.

Your milk can be cold or room temperature, I have done this both ways and the process has worked out well either way.

Step 1: Pour milk into the container.

Next add 1/4 teaspoon ( or 1/8 teaspoon if you are halving the recipe) of your culture and stir well with a wooden spoon. You do not want to use a metal spoon.

Now, add 1 drop of your liquid rennet or else dissolve 1 & 1/2 rennet tablets, into your 1/4 cup of water and mix to blend.

Take 2 Tablespoons (use 1 Tablespoon if you are halving the recipe) of this mixture, and add it to the milk. Stir well. Cover container with a cloth napkin or dish towel and secure with a rubber band.

Let your milk, culture and rennet sit for 24 hours.

Simple so far, right? You will let your milk mixture sit out for 24 hours. I just let mine sit on the counter in an out of the way spot but if you are short on space you can place it in your oven, just be sure not to "preheat" while your milk is in there! During this time your milk will thicken into curds.

If you want to jump-start the process & make it quickly, slowly heat instead in a porcelain-lined (Le-Cruset-type ware, also non-reactive) pot, stirring with a wooden spoon, until its blood-warm, like tepid bathwater. Do not overheat. Take off heat after adding rennet & water solution, cover & cool.

Soon you shall have "Curds and whey"!

The next day (Or in about an hour or two later that afternoon, if you heated it) you will want to (cut through in a criss-cross if wanted, &) drain your cheese curds from the whey which has separated during the 24 hour period. Place a large colander in a large bowl and line with a fine butter muslin, cheese cloth (I double or quadruple mine so the holes are thereby finer) or you can use a cotton cloth napkin, etc.

Carefully pour your curds into the colander, it should be jelled and have the consistency of a thick yogurt. You do not have to worry too much if they fall apart a little.

Tie up the corners of your cheese cloth to enclose the curds and be sure to keep the ends inside the colander or the whey will drip all over your counter.

You may need to pour off they whey into another container so that the colander doesn't sit "in" the whey and so it can finish dripping. You can save your whey for fermenting, protein for smoothies if you freeze them in ice-cube trays, they can be used in all kinds of cooking recipes, baking bread... or give it to your animals, they love it! Let your curds sit for another 24 hours, or overnight in the fridge, covered with a cloth.

This is the moment you have been waiting! Untie your cheese cloth and transfer your chevre to a clean bowl. Add 1 teaspoon of sea salt or kosher salt, (I love pink Himalayan salt personally) and blend well. Remember to use only 1/2 teaspoon if you have halved this recipe.

You can get creative and combine herbs and spices to your cheese or eat it plain! I like garlic, dill and chives, or parsley, sage, rosemary and thyme. I add a bit of extra-virgin olive oil even with the fresh herbs.... mmm! You can also mix with jam, purchased or homemade, or syrups like the rose one! It can go savory or sweet.

Zatar is another wonderful blend of Middle Eastern spices, including primarily driued thyme, that pairs perfectly with chevre. Traditionally it is mixed with olive oil and baked into the crust of flat bread but I like to just mix it into the cheese or top it off and eat it! Yum.

Store your cheese in small containers in the refrigerator. You can also freeze your chevre. Just allow it to thaw in the refrigerator for 24 to 48 hours before eating.

\*\*\*

What did I promise you about homemade bread, butter & cheese? Enjoy, with Love.

# Chapter 4: Keeping Small-Scale Livestock (Chickens, Goats, Rabbits); Beekeeping

Chickens are a delight to keep for many useful & practical reasons. They give fresh eggs (& meat if you are non-vegetarian), rich manure for garden fertilizer; they feast upon your kitchen scraps, a little grain (mostly during winter when natural food sources are more scarce), eat insects & other pests, & require very little care or cost other than the initial investment for hens, an optional rooster, & building supplies for the coop. You can use reclaimed or recycled materials as well for a virtually zero-cost coop. I have included a link to a chicken-coop building plan below.

Mother Earth News chimes in on the subject: "Eggs from backyard flocks are of a quality and nutritional density that those dependent on the supermarket can only dream of... Backyard flocks can contribute to self-sufficiency in more ways than simply putting food on the table. They offer bug control, tillage and great entertainment.

Poultry are incredible starter livestock for most homesteads, because their needs are easily and cheaply met, and the homesteader can start on a small scale.

One reason poultry are the easiest livestock is that their housing can be simple. All domesticated poultry are hardy and will do well if given protection from predators and the extremes of weather. Any housing that protects the birds from wind, rain and snow will be adequate for your flock. (Remember, too, their need for shade on the hottest summer days.) You should provide a minimum of 3 square feet per adult bird — 4 or 5 would be even better.

Chickens, guineas and turkeys all have an instinct to roost at night and will be more content if given perches to do so. Any structure that allows them to sleep perched above ground level will satisfy their urge to roost.

If there are laying hens in your flock, you should provide nests. I make my own (12 inches high and wide, 16 inches deep) and fill them with straw, leaves or other clean, soft material.

Almost any structure can serve satisfactorily for housing poultry. I strongly advise leaving an earth floor in the coop and covering it with a layer of organic matter such as clean straw.

All domestic poultry are quite cold hardy. They don't need added heat usually, as long as they are protected from the wind in the coldest weather. I make certain that their house is tight against drafts, while at the same time providing essential ventilation. Occasionally, cocks (males) suffer frostbite to their large combs and wattles (the red, fleshy protuberances on top of and hanging from their heads). If you live further north, you might want to consider breeds such as the chantecler, which have minimal combs and wattles that are almost impervious to frostbite."

I would encourage you to start with about 5-10 hens for egg-laying such as Rhode Island Reds, at a young breeding age, about 16 weeks I believe. You can find additional reading material to hatch & raise chicks from eggs, but it won't be covered here as we're starting simply as possible here, for you. Please do look into it though, as it is very rewarding & takes things to a deeper level of the homesteading arts!

Below are plans to build a small, moveable chicken/fowl coop:

Portable Mini Chicken Coop Plans, from Mother Earth News:

http://www.motherearthnews.com/diy/portable-chicken-mini-coop-plan.aspx#axzz34SIwC6V4

Goats are amazing to keep for milk, optional meat, & many breeds you can also collect & use the hair/wool as you would sheep's. Cashmere fiber is naturally from Kashmiri Goats, & Mohair fiber comes from Angora Goats. You can make many, many amazing artisan products from the milk of goats alone.... & they also help clear land from underbrush & "mow" the lawn! Their manure can also be used as an excellent fertilizer & ingredient in organic compost. Just make SURE their pen is extremely tight & escape-proof- they are notorious Houdini-like escape artists!

Rabbits are very easy to raise for fiber (angora rabbits are what angora fiber comes from), & optional fur/pelts & tender meat. They are easily cared for in hutches that can be outdoors most of the year or in a little well-ventilated shed, just be sure to keep them clean & dry, away from loud noises where they may startle & frighten easily, and plenty of water at all times besides good quantities of fresh greens such as clover, dandelions, & grain. There are many excellent rabbit hutch plans online as well.


Beekeeping in recent years has taken on a new importance: Besides local raw honey & beeswax, bee pollen & other prized health products from the bees, plus pollinating all your crops, there is another pressing reason we should all keep bees: They are now officially on the Endangered Species List, and need all the help, love & attention we can possibly spare to ensure even the safekeeping of the world's future food supply. This is a serious issue, and must be addressed on a personal level as we can, as well as a global one. Again, there are many hive plans & options online, as well as books devoted entirely to the subject, although I cannot recommend this book highly enough: "Swarm Traps & Bait Hives: The Easy Way To Get Bees For Free" by McCartney M Taylor. He actually teaches you to wild-snare bees for your farmstead & own personal use, its amazing. You can also purchase swarms of domesticated bees online. Also, planting native wildflowers to the region, as well as bee-friendly plants such as Scarlet Bee Balm to attract the honeybees to your homestead, is highly recommended & will help them recognize a safe haven & food source, with their sweetly-scented, brilliant red blossoms acting as a natural beacon.

# Chapter 5: Introduction To Probiotic Fermentation

"What on EARTH is Fermentation," you may ask. Many traditional & classic foods & beverages are, in fact, fermented: From alcoholic drinks like beer, wine, honey mead, etc., to many staples & culinary delights including pickles, cheese, tea & coffee, yogurt, chocolate, Korean pickled garlic & veggie Kimchi, German sauerkraut, Russian "kvass", Kefir (drinkable probiotic yogurt), & water kefir (natural homemade fermented soda), ancient Chinese fermented kombucha tea, San Francisco (& European) sourdough breads, vinegar, Asian soy sauces, tempeh, miso... & much, much more!!!!

In this day & age of overcooked, over processed methods, almost all the natural enzymes present in foods are destroyed. Our body needs these enzymes to properly digest our food & obtain the crucial nutrients, keeping our intestinal "good bacteria" flourishing, & warding off disease & illness. When we don't take these good, live enzymes in so we can get the most from our meals, it leads obviously to all manner of atrocities & illness. Adding enzymes & beneficial bacteria back into our diets & our bodies is exactly what we need, & our bodies crave them.

Here's what Casey Seidenburg of the Washington Post has to say on the subject:

"Why does this process [of fermentation] help people stay healthy?

Fermented foods aid in digestion and thus support the immune system.

— Imagine a fermented food as a partially digested food. For instance, many people have difficulty digesting the lactose in milk. When milk is fermented and becomes yogurt or kefir, the lactose is partially broken down so it becomes more digestible.

— Organic or lactic-acid fermented foods (such as dill pickles and sauerkraut) are rich in enzyme activity that aids in the breakdown of our food, helping us absorb the important nutrients we rely on to stay healthy.

— Fermented foods have been shown to support the beneficial bacteria in our digestive tract. In our antiseptic world with chlorinated water, antibiotics in our meat, our milk and our own bodies, and antibacterial everything, we could use some beneficial bacteria in our bodies.

— When our digestion is functioning properly and we are absorbing and assimilating all the nutrients we need, our immune system tends to be happy, and thus better equipped to wage war against disease and illness.

I am not claiming that fermented foods are a panacea, but I do believe these foods encourage effective digestion and — along with sleep, exercise and a nutrient-rich diet — help nurture a strong immune system.

Are you turned off by the idea of a fermented food? Don't be. Fermented foods are valued for their health benefits and as a means of food preservation, but they wouldn't have been part of our diets for so long if they weren't tasty as well. For some, a fermented, stinky cheese is a delicacy. And it pairs nicely with a glass of fermented red wine.

Incorporating fermented foods into your diet

To receive the health benefits and the flavors of fermented foods, you don't need to make an entire meal of them. Just a little bit will do. A spoonful of sauerkraut on your sausage offers benefits and adds flavor. So do a few sips of miso soup to begin a meal or a few pickles on a turkey sandwich.

Incorporating fermented foods into the diet is simple.

— Replace regular bread with a fresh sourdough variety.

— Choose kefir and yogurt over regular milk. Both work well in smoothies.

— Kombucha is a fermented drink found in many grocery stores.

— Look for naturally fermented vegetables such as pickled cucumbers, beets, onions, sauerkraut, salsa and kimchi. These are sold in the refrigerated section of your grocery store, not with the shelf-stable foods. Add a spoonful to any dish.

— Use miso to marinate fish or in soup.

— Add a tablespoon of fermented chutney to cooked meat.

— Use naturally fermented condiments (found in the refrigerated section of your grocery store). Because my kids love ketchup and would put it on everything if I allowed, I have started making my own using the recipe in the cookbook "Nourishing Traditions." My variety is fermented and thus has all the associated benefits, unlike most commercial ketchup, which is made with sugar or corn syrup and other additives.

— Look for a book about fermentation if you are inspired to try it yourself.

We have heard over and over again that we should eat as our ancestors ate. There is evidence that people have been fermenting foods since 3000 B.C., so if fermentation isn't going back to our food roots, I don't know what is."

One of my favorite authors on the subject of fermentation, and two of his books, are "Wild Fermentation" & "The Art of Fermentation" by Sandor Katz. Sandor was diagnosed with AIDS in the 80's and sub sequentially, miraculously healed himself through daily fermenting & eating live, probiotic fermented foods & drinks. His story is absolutely incredible, and his kitchen, full of bubbly crocks of this & of that, continues to inspire & heal many. Absolutely a must-read author if you want to explore fermentation beyond this book. In the meantime, I will give you several easy beginner's recipes to show you how to start fermenting living, raw probiotics for yourself & your family.

My absolute favorite source for probiotic cultures & starters, if you cannot find them locally from fellow homesteaders/fermenters, is Cultures For Health. http://www.culturesforhealth.com/ They have everything you can possibly need to get started & beyond with kombucha SCOBYs/"mothers", kefir grains, cheese making & yogurt making cultures, sourdough starters, & so much more!

Yogurt is an easy beginning project without having to buy starters or special equipment if you don't want to. All you need is some milk (raw is preferable, but pasteurized store bought is good too), a thermos or crockpot, & a couple tablespoons of a plain, store bought live-culture (such as activia, or an organic one preferably) yogurt to culture the new milk you're turning into yogurt. The milk needs heated to just blood-warm (life the cheese we made), & then the yogurt "starter culture" mixed in. It then needs covered (Ambient temperature can have an effect on the culturing process; in cold weather, wrap with a warmed towel for added insulation.), for 8-10 hours on average. When you check it the next morning, Behold! Your first homemade, cultured, live probiotic yogurt!!!

An additional wonder is that your crock pot can act as a one-pot container for heating and incubating the milk when making yogurt. And it really couldn't be any simpler.

*Crock Pot Yogurt*

Turn crock pot to low and pour in ½ gallon of milk (fresh cow, goat, etc. milk is preferable, but if not then try with store bought).

Heat on low for 2½ hours.

Turn crock pot off, and unplug it. Cool milk in the crock with the lid on for 3 hours.

After 3 hours, remove 1-2 cups of warmed milk and place in a bowl. To that milk, add starter culture or starter yogurt, according to the culture's instructions.

Thoroughly combine the milk and starter, mixing very well.

Pour the starter-milk mixture back into the crock pot with the rest of the milk and whisk thoroughly.

Place the cover back on the crock and wrap the entire crock pot in a thick bath towel or two.

Culture 8-12 hours or overnight.

After the culturing period, store in glass quart jars in refrigerator.

For optimum texture, refrigerate for at least 6 hours before using.

(*NOTE: Greek yogurt is regular yogurt, merely strained several hours through a cheesecloth set in a colander, which in turn is set inside a glass bowl. Experiment! You can also make yogurt cheese/farmer's cheese by pressing & straining in cheesecloth overnight- an amazing dessert cheese mixed with fresh berries or jam!)

\*\*\*

*Kombucha (Fermented Probiotic Tea) How-To*

"Kombucha" is a fermented tea drink that has been around for centuries, or more. The high concentration of b-vitamins, digestive enzymes, and glucaric acid in kombucha are credited with a variety of health effects, including detoxification, improved digestion, increased liver function and more.

Many Kombucha drinkers also report increased energy from regular consumption. Some studies have even shown that compounds like glucaric acid can help prevent cancer, though the evidence on this is limited. Interestingly, President Reagan reportedly drank kombucha daily as part of his regimen to battle stomach cancer when he was diagnosed in 1987 (He died in 2004 of old age).

Countries around the world, from China to Russia, value Kombucha for its health benefits, though few scientific studies have been done in the US. Despite this, Kombucha has gained popularity, especially in some parts of the country.

Kombucha is now available commercially, though prices range from $3-7 for a small bottle, or even more.

An entire gallon of Kombucha can be made at home for a dollar or less, and the process is very simple, really.

The culture that creates Kombucha is referred to as a "Mother" or a "SCOBY," which stands for "Symbiotic Colony of Bacteria and Yeast." There are several ways to obtain a SCOBY.

*How To Find a SCOBY (Starter) to Brew Kombucha

If you know someone who already brews Kombucha, ask them if they have an extra you could have, buy or barter for. A SCOBY reproduces itself and has a "baby" every few batches, so often someone who brews Kombucha will have extras.

You can order a SCOBY from a reputable online source such as Cultures for Health (that I mentioned with link, above). It will come in a dehydrated state with instructions for how to brew. They also have great tutorial videos on brewing Kombucha.

Grow your own. You will just need a bottle of organic, unflavored Kombucha, & plenty of patience. Prepare as below & put the bottle of premade kombucha in, in place of the mother.

Finding a SCOBY is often the most difficult part, as the actual making of Kombucha is pretty easy...

*How To Brew Kombucha*

You will need:

A gallon size glass jar

1 gallon (or a little less) of brewed sweetened tea, with a ratio of 1 cup organic sugar to 1 gallon of tea – must be cooled to room temperature!

1 Kombucha SCOBY or dehydrated SCOBY

A kitchen towel or coffee filter and a rubber band

Instructions:

[Note: It is very important that all materials and surfaces are very clean and that your hands have been washed before starting this process so only good bacteria goes into it!]

Prepare the tea (1 cup organic sugar in 1 gallon of brewed regular tea- decaf is ok too!) Use 3-4 family size tea bags or 8-10 regular size ones.

Let the tea cool and remove tea bags. Make sure that tea is completely cool before going on to next step.

Pour the tea into a gallon size glass jar, leaving at least an inch of room at the top.

Add 1 cup of liquid from a previous batch of Kombucha or from a store bought bottle of plain organic Kombucha.

Gently place the Kombucha SCOBY at the top of the liquid. It should float, but don't worry if it doesn't. Once you have put it in, don't put your hands into the tea to get it to float!

Cover the jar with a coffee filter, cloth napkin, or towel and secure with a strong rubber band.

Place in a warm location (around 70-75 degrees) and let sit from roughly 10 days depending on your preference (it will be less sweet and more potent the longer you leave it). You can taste-test it after a week.

When it is finished brewing, you can store in smaller jars or in another big jar with a lid and repeat the brewing process with the SCOBY to make more batches. Every 1-2 batches, the SCOBY will have a baby that can be used to make other batches or given away. Refrigerate after it is done to your taste, or it will continue to ferment further & get stronger & acidic/sour. Although some people like it strong that way, they will do daily "shots" of over-fermented kombucha for purely health purposes! As always, dear homesteading reader, experiment & have FUN!

# Chapter 6: Water Conservation, Alternative Energy Sources (Energy Independence)

According to Eartheasy.com, "In 1990, 30 states in the US reported 'water-stress' conditions. In 2000, the number of states reporting water-stress rose to 40. In 2009, the number rose to 45. There is a worsening trend in water supply nationwide. Taking measures at home to conserve water not only saves you money, it also is of benefit to the greater community.

Saving water at home does not require any significant cost outlay. Although there are water-saving appliances and water conservation systems such as rain barrels, drip irrigation and on-demand water heaters which are more expensive, the bulk of water saving methods can be achieved at little cost. For example, 75% of water used indoors is in the bathroom, and 25% of this is for the toilet. The average toilet uses 4 gallons per flush (gpf). You can invest in a ULF (ultra-low flush) toilet which will use only 2 gpf. But you can also install a simple tank bank, costing about $2, which will save .8 gpf. This saves 40% of what you would save with the ULF toilet. Using simple methods like tank banks, low-flow showerheads and faucet aerators you can retrofit your home for under$50."

1. Check faucets and pipes for leaks

A small drip from a worn faucet washer can waste 20 gallons of water per day. Larger leaks can waste hundreds of gallons.

2. Don't use the toilet as an ashtray or wastebasket

Every time you flush a cigarette butt, facial tissue or other small bit of trash, five to seven gallons of water is wasted.

3. Check your toilets for leaks

Put a little food coloring in your toilet tank. If, without flushing, the color begins to appear in the bowl within 30 minutes, you have a leak that should be repaired immediately. Most replacement parts are inexpensive and easy to install.

4. Use your water meter to check for hidden water leaks

Read the house water meter before and after a two-hour period when no water is being used. If the meter does not read exactly the same, there is a leak.

5. Install water-saving shower heads and low-flow faucet aerators

Inexpensive water-saving low-flow shower heads or restrictors are easy for the homeowner to install. Also, long, hot showers can use five to ten gallons every unneeded minute. Limit your showers to the time it takes to soap up, wash down and rinse off. "Low-flow" means it uses less than 2.5 gallons per minute.

You can easily install a Shower Start showerhead, or add a Shower Start converter to existing showerheads, which automatically pauses a running shower once it gets warm.

Also, all household faucets should be fit with aerators. This single best home water conservation method is also the cheapest!

6. Put plastic bottles or float booster in your toilet tank

To cut down on water waste, put an inch or two of sand or pebbles inside each of two plastic bottles to weigh them down. Fill the bottles with water, screw the lids on, and put them in your toilet tank, safely away from the operating mechanisms. Or, buy an inexpensive tank bank or float booster. This may save ten or more gallons of water per day.

Be sure at least 3 gallons of water remain in the tank so it will flush properly. If there is not enough water to get a proper flush, users will hold the lever down too long or do multiple flushes to get rid of waste. Two flushing's at 1.4 gallons is worse than a single 2.0 gallon flush. A better suggestion would be to buy an adjustable toilet flapper that allow for adjustment of their per flush use. Then the user can adjust the flush rate to the minimum per flush setting that achieves a single good flush each time.

For new installations, consider buying "low flush" toilets, which use 1 to 2 gallons per flush instead of the usual 3 to 5 gallons.

Replacing an 18 liter per flush toilet with an ultra-low volume (ULV) 6 liter flush model represents a 70% savings in water flushed and will cut indoor water use by about 30%.

## 7. Insulate your water pipes.

It's easy and inexpensive to insulate your water pipes with pre-slit foam pipe insulation. You'll get hot water faster plus avoid wasting water while it heats up.

## 8. Take shorter showers.

One way to cut down on water use is to turn off the shower after soaping up, then turn it back on to rinse. A four-minute shower uses approximately 20 to 40 gallons of water.

## 9. Turn off the water after you wet your toothbrush

There is no need to keep the water running while brushing your teeth. Just wet your brush and fill a glass for mouth rinsing.

## 10. Rinse your razor in the sink

Fill the sink with a few inches of warm water. This will rinse your razor just as well as running water, with far less waste of water.

## 11. Use your dishwasher and clothes washer for only full loads

Automatic dishwashers and clothes washers should be fully loaded for optimum water conservation. Most makers of dishwashing soap recommend not pre-rinsing dishes which is a big water savings.

With clothes washers, avoid the permanent press cycle, which uses an added 20 liters (5 gallons) for the extra rinse. For partial loads, adjust water levels to match the size of the load. Replace old clothes washers. New Energy Star rated washers use 35 - 50% less water and 50% less energy per load. If you're in the market for a new clothes washer, consider buying a water-saving frontload washer.

## 12. Minimize use of kitchen sink garbage disposal units

In-sink 'garburators' require lots of water to operate properly, and also add considerably to the volume of solids in a septic tank which can lead to maintenance problems. Start a compost pile as an alternate method of disposing food waste.

## 13. When washing dishes by hand, don't leave the water running for rinsing

If you have a double-basin, fill one with soapy water and one with rinse water. If you have a single-basin sink, gather washed dishes in a dish rack and rinse them with a spray device or a painful of hot water. Dual-swivel aerators are available to make this easier. If using a dishwasher, there is usually no need to pre-rinse the dishes.

## 14. Don't let the faucet run while you clean vegetables

Just rinse them in a stoppered sink or a pan of clean water. Use a dual-setting aerator.

## 15. Keep a bottle of drinking water in the fridge.

Running tap water to cool it off for drinking water is wasteful. Store drinking water in the fridge in a safe drinking bottle. If you are filling water bottles to bring along on outdoor hikes, consider buying a Life Straw personal water filter which enables users to drink water safely from rivers or lakes or any available body of water.

Water conservation in the yard and garden...

## 16. Plant drought-resistant lawns, shrubs and plants

If you are planting a new lawn, or over seeding an existing lawn, use drought-resistant grasses such as the new "Eco-Lawn".

Many beautiful shrubs and plants thrive with far less watering than other species. Replace herbaceous perennial borders with native plants. Native plants will use less water and be more resistant to local plant diseases. Consider applying the principles of xeriscaping for a low-maintenance, drought resistant yard.

Plant slopes with plants that will retain water and help reduce runoff.

Group plants according to their watering needs.


## 17. Put a layer of mulch around trees and plants

Mulch will slow evaporation of moisture while discouraging weed growth. Adding 2 - 4 inches of organic material such as compost or bark mulch will increase the ability of the soil to retain moisture. Press the mulch down around the drip line of each plant to form a slight depression which will prevent or minimize water runoff.

For information about different mulch materials and their best use, click here.


## 18. Don't water the gutter

Position your sprinklers so water lands on the lawn or garden, not on paved areas. Also, avoid watering on windy days.


## 19. Water your lawn only when it needs it

A good way to see if your lawn needs watering is to step on the grass. If it springs back up when you move, it doesn't need water. If it stays flat, the lawn is ready for watering. Letting the grass grow taller (to 3") will also promote water retention in the soil.

Most lawns only need about 1" of water each week. During dry spells, you can stop watering altogether and the lawn will go brown and dormant. Once cooler weather arrives, the morning dew and rainfall will bring the lawn back to its usual vigor. This may result in a brown summer lawn, but it saves a lot of water.


## 20. Deep-soak your lawn

When watering the lawn, do it long enough for the moisture to soak down to the roots where it will do the most good. A light sprinkling can evaporate quickly and tends to encourage shallow root systems. Put an empty tuna can on your lawn - when it's full, you've watered about the right amount. Visit our natural lawn care page for more information.

21. Water during the early parts of the day; avoid watering when it's windy

Early morning is generally better than dusk since it helps prevent the growth of fungus. Early watering, and late watering, also reduce water loss to evaporation. Watering early in the day is also the best defense against slugs and other garden pests. Try not to water when it's windy - wind can blow sprinklers off target and speed evaporation.

22. Add organic matter and use efficient watering systems for shrubs, flower beds and lawns

Adding organic material to your soil will help increase its absorption and water retention. Areas which are already planted can be 'top dressed' with compost or organic matter.

You can greatly reduce the amount of water used for shrubs, beds and lawns by:

- The strategic placement of soaker hoses

- installing a rain barrel water catchment system

- installing a simple drip-irrigation system

Avoid over-watering plants and shrubs, as this can actually diminish plant health and cause yellowing of the leaves.

When hand watering, use a variable spray nozzle for targeted watering.

23. Don't run the hose while washing your car

Clean the car using a pail of soapy water. Use the hose only for rinsing - this simple practice can save as much as 150 gallons when washing a car. Use a spray nozzle when rinsing for more efficient use of water. Better yet, use a waterless car washing system; there are several brands, such as Eco Touch, which are now on the market.

24. Use a broom, not a hose, to clean driveways and sidewalks

25. Check for leaks in pipes, hoses, faucets and couplings

Leaks outside the house may not seem as bad since they're not as visible. But they can be just as wasteful as leaks indoors. Check frequently to keep them drip-free. Use hose washers at spigots and hose connections to eliminate leaks.

Water conservation comes naturally when everyone in the family is aware of its importance, and parents take the time to teach children some of the simple water-saving methods around the home which can make a big difference.

Collecting Rainwater is a useful skill & habit to add to your slew of homesteading capabilities, & can be used to water the lawn & gardens, wash the car or the dog, and more. Not recommended for drinking unless it first would be additionally purified after collection, but you can learn to do that too so you have the wisdom for it in case of power outage... That is the insurmountable beauty of Homesteading skills: Even if you don't end up using them every day in your routine, once you possess the knowledge of it, you will carry it with you for a lifetime & can pass it on to others as well who may need it. Below is an excellent resource from the Pennsylvania State Government about collecting rainwater for the watershed project, including plans, here:

http://www.lccd.org/watershed/Rain_Barrel_Brochure.pdf

Alternative Energy

According to Altenergy.org, "Everyday, the world produces carbon dioxide that is released to the earth's atmosphere and which will still be there in one hundred years' time.

This increased content of Carbon Dioxide increases the warmth of our planet and is the main cause of the so called "Global Warming Effect". One answer to global warming is to replace and retrofit current technologies with alternatives that have comparable or better performance, but do not emit carbon dioxide.

We call this Alternate energy.

By 2050, one-third of the world's energy will need to come from solar, wind, and other renewable resources. Who says? British Petroleum and Royal Dutch Shell, two of the world's largest oil companies. Climate change, population growth, and fossil fuel depletion mean that renewables will need to play a bigger role in the future than they do today.

Alternative energy refers to energy sources that have no undesired consequences such for example fossil fuels or nuclear energy. Alternative energy sources are renewable and are thought to be "free" energy sources. They all have lower carbon emissions, compared to conventional energy sources. These include Biomass Energy, Wind Energy, Solar Energy, Geothermal Energy, Hydroelectric Energy sources. Combined with the use of recycling, the use of clean alternative energies such as the home use of solar power systems will help ensure man's survival into the 21st century and beyond."

In the Homesteading world, solar power is the best-known & used of these, although they are ALL worth researching to see what is best for you to possibly incorporate. Today's solar panels, although a usually significant investment, are actually bombproof, and often come with a 25 year warranty or more. Your solar panels may outlive you. They are also modular—you can start with a small system and expand it over time. Solar panels are light (weighing about 20 pounds), so if you move you can take the system with you. There are also ways to build your own, it is amazing!

Can you imagine never paying another electric bill again, or even being paid/reimbursed by the electric company for the extra energy you create & sell back to them, with your very own solar panels, and/or windmill? Researching this for yourself is your first step ultimately toward energy independence, and a cleaner, safer, greener world.

# Conclusion

Thank you again for downloading this book!

I hope this book was able to help you to realize just how easy it is to start homesteading & not be afraid to just plunge in & start!

The next step is to teach & inform others about how easy it is to get "Back to the Basics" too in any way we can, as we learn & experiment more on our own journey towards self-sufficiency.

Finally, if you enjoyed this book, please take the time to share your thoughts and post a review on Amazon. It'd be greatly appreciated!

Let us "BE the Change we want to see in the World", as Ghandi fondly said.

Thank you, and best of luck on your Journey of Everyday Homesteading Bliss!